# GROW YOUR OWN
# SUNFLOWERS

BY LISA J. AMSTUTZ

PEBBLE
a capstone imprint

Published by Pebble, an imprint of Capstone
1710 Roe Crest Drive, North Mankato, Minnesota 56003
capstonepub.com

Copyright © 2025 by Capstone. All rights reserved. No part of this publication may be reproduced in whole or in part, or stored in a retrieval system, or transmitted in any form or by any means, electronic, mechanical, photocopying, recording, or otherwise, without written permission of the publisher.

Library of Congress Cataloging-in-Publication Data
Names: Amstutz, Lisa J., author.
Title: Grow your own sunflowers / by Lisa J. Amstutz.
Description: North Mankato, Minnesota : Pebble, an imprint of Capstone, [2025] | Series: Pebble maker | Audience: Ages 5-8 | Audience: Grades 2-3 | Summary: "Encourage a love of nature and science with this book. Readers learn step-by-step how to grow and care for sunflowers. Then they learn about harvesting the seeds and how to make a bird feeder out of the dried flower"— Provided by publisher.
Identifiers: LCCN 2024020617 (print) | LCCN 2024020618 (ebook) | ISBN 9780756589493 (hardcover) | ISBN 9780756589653 (paperback) | ISBN 9780756589530 (pdf) | ISBN 9780756589677 (kindle edition) | ISBN 9780756589660 (epub)
Subjects: LCSH: Sunflowers—Juvenile literature. | Gardening—Juvenile literature.
Classification: LCC QK495.C74 A47 2025 (print) | LCC QK495.C74 (ebook) | DDC 583/.983—dc23/eng/20240607
LC record available at https://lccn.loc.gov/2024020617
LC ebook record available at https://lccn.loc.gov/2024020618

Editorial Credits
Editor: Erika L. Shores; Designer: Heidi Thompson; Media Researcher: Jo Miller; Production Specialist: Tori Abraham

Image Credits
Getty Images: annick vanderschelden photography, 19, claylib, 15, Stephanie Nantel, 17, Yulia Bliznyakova, 23 (bottom); Shutterstock: Artem Stepanov, 7 (bottom left), 11 (right), Bogdan Wankowicz, cover (bottom left), 12, Chamois huntress, 21, Hunter Leader, 23 (top right), Kai3999, cover (right), La Huertina De Toni, 18, Lotus Images, cover (top left), 6 (bottom), Mallinka1, 23 (top left), New Africa, 10, onair, 7 (bottom right), 11 (plate), Philip Bird LRPS CPAGB, 5, Sergio33, back cover, 1, Taras Garkusha, cover (middle left), 9 (soil and pot), 11 (pot), 13 (pot), Tavarius, 13 (plant), Thammasak Lek, 6 (top), 9 (trowel), Valery Kraynov, 7 (top)

The publisher and the author shall not be liable for any damages allegedly arising from the information in this book, and they specifically disclaim any liability from the use or application of any of the contents of this book.

Any additional websites and resources referenced in this book are not maintained, authorized, orsponsored by Capstone. All product and company names are trademarks™ or registered® trademarks of their respective holders.

Printed and bound in China. 6097

# TABLE OF CONTENTS

Sky-High Plants . . . . . . . . . . . . . . . . . . . . . . . . . . . 4

What You Need . . . . . . . . . . . . . . . . . . . . . . . . . . . 6

What You Do . . . . . . . . . . . . . . . . . . . . . . . . . . . . 8

Take It Further . . . . . . . . . . . . . . . . . . . . . . . . . . 20

Behind the Science . . . . . . . . . . . . . . . . . . . . . . . 22

Glossary . . . . . . . . . . . . . . . . . . . . . . . . . . . . . . 24

About the Author . . . . . . . . . . . . . . . . . . . . . . . . 24

Words in **BOLD** are in the glossary.

# SKY-HIGH PLANTS

Tall sunflowers look pretty.

You can grow your own.

Wait for the **frost date** to pass.

Then plant seeds in your garden.

You can start the plants in pots too.

This gives them a head start.

Read on to learn how!

# WHAT YOU NEED

- two sunflower seeds
- potting soil
- trowel
- **peat pot**
- dish or tray
- clean spray bottle
- water
- a sunny spot indoors

# WHAT YOU DO

## STEP 1

Use the trowel to scoop some potting soil. Fill the peat pot. Leave some space at the top.

Push two seeds into the soil. Plant them a half-inch deep. Cover them with soil.

## STEP 2

Fill the spray bottle with water. Spray the soil until it is damp. Set the pot on a dish or tray to catch leaks. Put it in a sunny spot.

Check the soil each day.

Mist with water if it feels dry.

But don't water it too much!

## STEP 3

The seeds will **sprout** in 7 to 10 days. Wait until they are a few inches tall. Then set the pot outside in the sun. Bring it in after a few hours. For a week, set the pot out longer each day.

## STEP 4

Now it's time for the big move. Find a sunny spot. A garden or flower bed is a good place. Dig a hole there. Make it big enough to hold the pot.

Put the pot in the hole. Press soil around it. This will hold it in place. Water it until the soil is damp.

# STEP 5

Now watch your plant grow! Pull weeds around it. Water if the soil gets too dry. The plant will grow tall. In a few months, sunflowers will bloom.

# STEP 6

Let the flowers dry on the **stalk**.

Then you can gather the seeds.

Sunflower seeds are good to eat. Crack open the **hull**. There is a **kernel** inside. Roast the kernels in the oven with oil and salt. Ask an adult to help.

# TAKE IT FURTHER

Turn your sunflower into a bird feeder. Cut off the flower, leaving some of the stalk. Poke a hole through the stalk. Push a string through the hole. Tie it on a tree branch or fence. Watch the birds come!

# BEHIND THE SCIENCE

We need food to live and grow. Plants do too! But they do not eat like we do. They make their own food.

Leaves take in light and air. Roots soak in water and **nutrients**. Plants use these to make food.

# GLOSSARY

**frost date** (FROST DAYT)—the date when the last frost comes in an area

**hull** (HUL)—the outer part of a seed

**kernel** (KUR-nuhl)—the inner part of a seed

**nutrients** (NOO-tree-uhnts)—parts of food, like vitamins, that are used for growth

**peat pot** (PEET POT)—a small flowerpot in which a plant can be grown and then replanted without having to be removed

**sprout** (SPROUT)—to start to grow

**stalk** (STOCK)—the stem of a plant

# ABOUT THE AUTHOR

Lisa J. Amstutz is the author of more than 150 children's books on topics ranging from applesauce to zebra mussels. An ecologist by training, she enjoys sharing her love of nature with kids. Lisa lives on a small farm with her family.